BAD BABY BEAR

by Hertha James

Can you spot Bad Baby Bear?

A Storybook for You to Illustrate

Powerword Publications

herthamuddyhorse@gmail.com

hertha.james@xtra.co.nz

Copyright © text 2023 Hertha James

Each book in the series,
For Budding Artists and Illustrators,
has nine pages of text and a blank page
alongside for the artist.

Edited by Bonnie Boon
Cover, title page, p 5 and p 24 images by Hertha James

ISBN 978-1-7385915-0-3

USING THIS BOOK

The book has a blank page for illustration alongside each page of text, and additional space for the artist on the text pages.

The idea is to have fun with any drawing style(s) that you like or want to practice.

The paper is not suitable for watercolour or felt pen. Pencil, colored pencils, charcoal pencils, wax crayons, pastels, and ink will work nicely.

Your focus might be stick figures, faces with expressions, clothing/fashion, cartoon drawing, closeups or wider scenes, bird's eye view, caricature, photorealism,

You may want to practice quick sketching, line drawing, doodling, figure drawing, gesture drawing, perspective.

You may want to play with shading techniques (hatching, stippling, scribbling, smudging) to create shadow, texture, and blending.

You may want to draw digitally, print out, and glue into the book.

You could find, or set up, scenes to photograph, print out, and paste into the book.

The series includes these titles:

Jack Defrosting is a humorous tale about a boy who must solve a dilemma. Suitable for reluctant readers.

Mystery of the Garden Gnomes tells the story of a garden brought back to life.

Bad Baby Bear (this book) is a retelling of 'Goldilocks and the Three Bears' from the Baby Bear's point of view.

Cindy is a modernized re-telling of 'Cinderella'.

Slip Sliding Away takes us through a trauma brought on by global warming.

Boo the Rescue Greyhound is about a girl who is excited to adopt a dog. She trains the dog well and they help solve a mystery.

The Cow Shows How is a story about how a girl overcomes her fear of giving a speech to her English class.

The Un-Wily Hare is a re-telling of 'The Tortoise and the Hare' story set in the real world.

Worm Rescue is a true story about worms in trouble given a new life in a new garden.

Look out for more titles to come.

For Ada, who has the biggest of bear collections.

Bad Baby Bear

Baby Bear was trying hard to annoy his parents. Rather than eating his porridge, he jumped around the room, leaping from bed to bed. Baby Bear often wondered if Ma and Pa Bear were really his parents. Why was his fur a light golden color rather than the black or brown of a respectable bear? He wondered if his parents liked him. They were cross with him so often.

It wasn't his fault that he wasn't hungry. "Let's go for a walk," he shouted. He was angry that Ma and Pa wouldn't let him play in the forest by himself.

His parents finally agreed to go for a walk before they had their breakfast. He raced out in front of them and climbed a tree. As Ma and Pa got closer, he raced to another tree to climb.

Suddenly Baby Bear saw a movement in the forest to his right. He caught a glimpse of golden hair trailing out of a green bonnet. "Wow," he whispered, and shimmied further up the tree to get a better look. "Someone has hair the same color as mine!"

Baby Bear forgot all about his parents. He watched from the tree until the golden hair moved out of sight. It was heading toward their house. He climbed down and followed, dodging from tree to tree. It was a girl, stopping to touch a mushroom here, smelling a flower there.

When she saw his house, she stopped and stared. "I wonder who lives here?" she said out loud.

"I do!" said Baby Bear stepping out from behind a tree.

"Oh my. Aren't you cute," she said.

Baby Bear was so enchanted with her blond hair that he decided to ignore that comment. Cute was not how he saw himself.

"Look, we have the same color hair,"
he said excitedly.

"So we do!" she exclaimed. "My name
is Goldilocks. What's your name?"

Baby Bear thought quickly. He needed
a good hip name. "Eric," he said.

"Pleased to meet you, Eric. Could I
come into your house for a drink of
water?"

"Sure," said Baby Bear, opening the
door.

"What a lovely little house," Goldilocks exclaimed. "But it does smell a bit like, well, bears. What's this goop on the plates?"

"Porridge," said Baby Bear. "You can have some if you like."

"Okay," said Goldilocks, and sampled the porridge in each of the three bowls. "Wow, the stuff in this smallest bowl is the sweetest." She polished off Baby Bear's bowl of porridge. To keep her company, Baby Bear ate half of his mother's porridge after adding more sugar.

"Want to play jumping from chair to bed to chair to bed to chair to bed?" Baby Bear asked.

"Fun!" Goldilocks shouted, pulling off her bonnet and taking the first leap, breaking the smallest chair.

Baby Bear couldn't stop looking at her gorgeous gold curls. "Do you think we can be friends and play together in the forest?" he asked.

"Sure. If your parents let you out to play. I've seen them in the forest. They are rather big!"

"What's going on here?" roared Pa Bear.

"What have you done?" said Ma Bear, surveying the spilled porridge, the broken chair, and the rumpled beds.

"I have a new friend," Baby Bear said grandly. "Look, our hair is the same color."

"I'm sorry about the mess," Goldilocks said, using her best smile. "I'll help clean it up."

"I should think so," growled Pa Bear.

"Your hair is lovely," sighed Ma Bear. "Baby Bear is so easily spotted in the forest with his blond fur.

We worry about him going out alone."

Goldilocks thought about this for a moment.

"My name is Goldilocks. Everyone in the forest knows me and I'm quite safe playing by myself. Maybe he can come out to play with me."

"And I want to be called Goldilocks too," Baby Bear shouted.

"No," said Goldilocks, I will call you Tawny, like a lion."

"Yay, my name is Tawny," yelled Baby Bear, giving Goldilocks a big hug. "When can we go out to play?"

ABOUT THE AUTHOR

Hertha James is the author of sixteen books about training horses with positive reinforcement, available via Amazon.

After a career as a zookeeper and animal handler on film sets, she taught high school Science and Biology for many years.

Her writing also includes:

- Extensive write-on resources for learning science vocabulary, which are highly popular in many schools.
- For young readers, a four-book series about horses published by Pinnacle Press.
- A series of three books introducing students to working in a science lab, published by Essential Resources.

The author's husband playing with their young bears during their movie-making career.